WORDS *of* HOPE *and* HEALING

SYMPATHY
and
CONDOLENCES

What to Say *and* Write
to Convey Your Support
After a Loss

Alan D. Wolfelt, Ph.D.

Companion
PRESS

An imprint of the Center for Loss and Life Transition | Fort Collins, Colorado

Companion Press is an imprint of the Center for Loss and Life Transition, 3735 Broken Bow Road, Fort Collins, Colorado 80526.

26 25 24 23 22 21   6 5 4 3 2 1

ISBN: 978-1-61722-305-1

CONTENTS

WELCOME

"All I ever wanted was to reach out and touch another human being, not just with my hands but with my heart."

— Tahereh Mafi

Someone you care about has suffered a significant life loss. What do you say to them?

You want to let them know you're sorry and that you're thinking about them. You want your genuine concern to come across. So how do you put your feelings into the right words—words that will help them feel acknowledged and supported?

Expressing condolences is so important, but it's often tricky. While there are no hard-and-fast rules that apply to all unique grievers and loss circumstances, there are concepts and guidelines that can help you become a better condolence-giver.

My hope is that this little book will find a home in your notecard drawer or on your electronic device of choice.

Whenever you're not sure what to say or write in a loss situation, I invite you to pull it out and page through it. You'll find tips and suggestions that will help you connect with more confidence and warmth.

Thank you for caring. Thank you for being someone who wants to help. Your loved ones and acquaintances are lucky to have you in their circle of support.

THE IMPORTANCE OF SUPPORTING PEOPLE IN GRIEF

"Too often we underestimate the power of a touch, a smile, a kind word, a listening ear, an honest compliment, or the smallest act of caring, all of which have the potential to turn a life around."

— Leo Buscaglia

Our culture isn't very good at grief. We often make grievers feel like they have to keep their grief private—invisible and locked up inside them. We also tend to imply they should be embarrassed about or ashamed of openly mourning. But the truth is that grief is normal and necessary, and so is expressing it honestly.

The term "condolence" is from the Latin word *condolere*, meaning "to grieve or suffer with another." That's what we're doing when we share our condolences. We're letting people in grief know that we feel for them. We're bearing witness to and honoring their authentic loss and pain.

The timing of condolences matters. We give them shortly after a loss. Why? Because for the mourner, social recognition is necessary for them to even set off on their mourning journeys. I always say that affirmation of a loss precedes any movement toward integrating the loss. In my forty years of grief counseling experience, people whose losses aren't acknowledged quickly and sufficiently enough by others often remain stuck in shock, numbness, and denial. They have a lingering sense of surrealness, and they sometimes tell me they think they're going crazy. All of these are normal early grief feelings, but with good, compassionate public acknowledgment and support, they start to soften, allowing grievers to fully acknowledge the reality themselves and truly feel and embrace their necessary grief.

So condolences are the first step in what can and should be a long-term commitment to supporting the grieving people we care about. A bit later we'll talk more about the importance of following up (see A Suggested Contact Timeline, page 42), but for now I'll just say that offering your condolences is like opening a door. When you genuinely let someone know you see them and their pain, you're signaling that you're one of the helpers willing to step inside their grief with them.

For grievers, the more helpers they have in that room alongside them, the better.

SYMPATHY OR EMPATHY?

"Empathy is full presence to what's alive in
the other person at this moment."
— John Cunningham

Many people use the words "sympathy" and "empathy" interchangeably. Yet there's an important difference between the two. Understanding this difference will make you a better helper.

When you're sympathetic to someone else, you are noticing and feeling concern for their circumstances, usually at a distance. You're "feeling sorry" for them. You are feeling "pity" for them. You're passively looking at their situation from the outside, and you are acknowledging the distress passively. You may be offering a simple solution, platitude, or distraction. Sometimes sympathy even includes a touch of judgment or superiority.

Sympathy is "feeling for" someone else.
Empathy, on the other hand, is about making an emotional connection. It is a more active process—one in which you

try to understand and feel the other person's experience from the inside out rather than imposing meaning from the outside in.

When you offer empathy, you're not judging the person or the circumstances. You are not offering simple solutions. Instead, you're making yourself vulnerable to the person's ever-changing thoughts, feelings, and circumstances by looking for connections to similar thoughts, feelings, and circumstances inside you. You are being present to the other person and allowing yourself to be taught by them.

Empathy is "feeling with" someone else.
Empathy is communicated when you respond at the emotional, feelings level of the mourner. You reach the mourner where they are, being careful not to bring judgment or a need to get them to "let go" and "move on." This dependable quality of empathy is what seems to free mourners to open their hearts and mourn from the inside out. You will know you are actively empathizing when the mourner trusts you, opens up to you, and feels you are trying to truly understand.

It's easier to be sympathetic, but it's more helpful to the mourner if you're empathetic. This book is entitled *Sympathy and Condolences* because those are the terms we as a culture use to describe the socially recognized rituals of reaching out to others after a loss. These are critical rituals, but as you practice them and improve your condolence skills, I hope you will remember that whenever possible you want to offer empathy, not sympathy, especially if you personally know the mourner.

LOSSES DESERVING OF YOUR EMPATHY

Depending on your age and life circumstances, you yourself may have experienced a number of losses of various kinds already. Which caused you deep, lasting grief? Which were sharply painful but maybe hurt a lot for a shorter length of time? Which created nagging worry, disappointment, or unease?

Grief may be different for different kinds of losses, but it's always difficult and deserving of empathy. So when you're wondering if you should say something to a friend or loved one about a relatively "minor" or ambiguous loss in their life, I hope you'll remember to err on the side of compassion.

Here's a good rule of thumb: If it hurts, it needs to be acknowledged and supported.

In addition to the death of a loved one, here are some common life losses and transitions that are always painful and thus deserving of your empathy:

- divorce

- break-ups

- illness

- estrangement or physical separation from a loved one

- loss of a pet

- "burst bubbles" (realizations that cherished people or things were not what the person believed, hoped, or dreamed them to be)

- betrayals

- abuse

- lost or broken dreams

- traumatic accidents or events

- leaving a home

- financial loss

- job change or loss

This isn't an exhaustive list, of course—just some thoughts to get you started. The idea is that if your friends and loved ones are going through any kind of loss or transition, they need and deserve your condolences and support.

ACTIVELY LISTENING

"Many people do not listen with the intent to understand.
They listen with the intent to reply."

— Stephen R. Covey

Before we dive into suggestions about what to say and what
not to say, I also want to advocate for the critical importance
of active listening. Because the truth is that what you say
or write to convey your support after a loss is often less
important than how you listen.

When you are talking to others, do you not only hear but
actively listen?

Active listening means listening with the intent not only to
cognitively understand everything that is being said but also
to feel what is being said. It means giving your undivided
attention and focus. It means paying attention to both verbal
and nonverbal cues. And it also means communicating a
high degree of attention and focus back to the other person.

Renowned Buddhist monk and teacher Thich Nhat Hanh calls it "deep listening." Here's what he says about it:

> *Deep listening is the kind of listening that can help relieve the suffering of the other person. You can call it compassionate listening. You listen with only one purpose: to help him or her empty his heart. And if you remember that you are helping him or her to suffer less, and then even if he says things full of wrong perceptions, full of bitterness, you are still capable to listen with compassion. One hour like that can bring transformation and healing.*

In addition to being mindful of your body language, tone of voice, and eye contact, deep or active listening during a conversation about loss means keeping your mouth closed most of the time and your ears open all of the time.

When I was first being trained as a counselor, I thought it was my job to make the mourner feel better. But with time, experience, and good supervision, I began to realize that my role was not to take the pain of grief away but instead to be present to it. I remember my mentor, Dr. Ken Dimick, saying to me, "Always start with your mouth closed and your ears open."

This advice applies to you, too. In face-to-face encounters or on the phone, your job as a condolence-giver is not to take away the pain but instead to be present to it. While you may be a giver of a brief sympathy or condolence message, your most important role is as witness and receiver. And that requires active, empathetic listening.

THREE LEVELS OF COMMUNICATION

When you're communicating with someone who is grieving, it might help you to consider that the exchange is actually happening on several levels:

1. information
2. emotion
3. meaning

The exchange of information is the communication about the facts of what happened (including when and how, etc.) to the person who died. The exchange of emotion, on the other hand, is where your active listening and empathy skills come in. You're not only learning about the information, you're communicating back your emotional support with your words, body language, tone of voice, and more. And the exchange of meaning begins to happen when the mourner begins to feel truly understood and supported. The most effective sympathies and condolences, especially in person or over the phone, achieve all three levels of communication.

YOUR FIRST CONTACT

"There's nothing more vital to the bond you share with someone else than simply being there for them."
— Suman Rai

Again, when it comes to extending condolences, timing matters.

I suggest that it's best to reach out to a grieving person or family as soon as you can—within a day or two of the loss if possible, or, if you don't hear about the loss immediately, within a day or two of learning about it. The first moment you feel that pang of sorrow and empathy—that's the time to respond. Your natural impulse is to feel compassion, so leverage that impulse to express it as well.

If the loss is a death and there will soon be a public visitation, funeral, or memorial service that you will attend, it may be appropriate for you to hold your condolences until then, especially if you're not a close family member or friend. But for most significant losses, an immediate response is best.

The first time you see or reach out to a grieving person is usually the most difficult moment. How you handle this encounter will often set the tone for how the mourner perceives your capacity to be supportive.

Below, I've listened the methods of extending condolences in order of preference. In general, the more personal and proximate, the better. Also, keep in mind that you don't have to choose just one. The most effective, helpful support plan (see page 42) will typically include more than one type of contact. You might stop by in person, for example, then follow up with a phone call in a day or two then send a sympathy card.

IN PERSON

Whenever possible and appropriate for the loss situation, reach out in person first. This is the most human way to offer your empathy and support—with your physical presence, especially if you know the griever well and it's a significant loss. You may think, "Oh, I don't want to bother them right now…" But the truth is that this feeling is often more about your own discomfort than their potential inconvenience.

What's more, you may be overestimating the number of people who are there to support the mourner in person. Don't assume that they have lots of friends and family members at their side in the immediate aftermath of a loss, because all too often this is not the case.

Stop by the mourner's house with a card and casserole or food item. If they can't come to the door—that's OK. You can leave what you've brought, and they will still be comforted knowing you made the effort.

If the grieving person is an acquaintance you see regularly— at work, for example, or church—please remember that it's your responsibility to approach them. Seek them out to bring up the subject and offer your condolences. The same convention applies out and about. If you run into them by happenstance, social etiquette dictates that you broach the subject first in the conversation.

Here's a second good rule of thumb: When in doubt, reach out.

WHAT ABOUT "PRIVATE" LOSSES?

Expressing sympathy and condolences for seemingly private or sensitive types of losses can feel especially delicate.

If someone you know had a miscarriage, for example, or has recently become estranged from a close family member, it can be difficult to know how or if you should be extending your condolences. Other losses considered sensitive or confidential might include separation from a spouse or partner, a life-threatening or chronic-illness diagnosis, a major financial or job loss, infertility, drug abuse or overdose, and many more.

Offering empathy for these types of invisible losses does call for extra caution and discretion. Whether your outreach will be seen as kind or intrusive will likely depend on how close your relationship is with the person who is grieving as well as their unique personality.

Still, what I urge you to remember most of all is that grief is almost always under-supported in our culture. The more openly we talk about our losses, and the more directly and compassionately we offer our presence and support to those who are no doubt grieving, the more we will evolve toward being a community that values emotional intelligence and kindness.

> *"If we share our story with someone who responds with empathy and understanding, shame can't survive."*
>
> — Brené Brown

So don't be afraid of being the rare helper who reaches out despite any uncertainty. It's OK to be tentative and even vague as you develop more trust with the person. If you're able to strike up a meaningful conversation in which you share some of your own recent struggles, the other person might do the same. You can also broach the subject indirectly, opening the door to fuller disclosure. Simply asking, "How have you been doing?" with generous genuineness and empathy can be enough to get the ball rolling.

Even better, when appropriate I suggest that you ask the potential "secret" or quiet griever, "How are you surviving?" It's often more effective because "How are you doing?" is such a stock politeness that it often invites mutual pretense. When they're asked "How are you doing?", people are trained to answer, "Oh, I'm fine"—whether they're actually fine or not. On the other hand, "How are you surviving?" is a different enough way of asking the question that it often breaks through to the truth. It conveys that you are someone who really and truly wants to know how they are doing.

And don't discount the power of a personal note. You can send a "thinking of you" card, email, or text at any time, offering generalized encouragement and support while avoiding point-blank mention of what has happened. This approach, too, may well open the door to deeper disclosure and conversation.

If the sensitive loss is publicly known information, on the other hand—a house fire, say, or a publicized job layoff—I would be more direct. You might gently say, "I'm so sorry you were affected by the downsizing at Company Name," for example. This gives the other person the opportunity to share whatever they'd like to share and you the opportunity to listen. And that's a giant meaningful step in the right direction.

ON THE PHONE

The next best thing to a face-to-face visit is a personal phone call. Your voice and listening skills will convey your empathy as much or more than the particular words you speak. Remember—it's more about listening than talking. Please refrain from talking about yourself or offering advice unless it's asked for.

If the loss was significant and you feel close to the person, call as soon as you can. If you have to leave a voicemail, that's OK. Leave a message and then try calling again the next day. If you still can't reach the person by phone, try sending a text or email to follow up.

ON A VIDEO CHAT

Video calls have become as common as voice calls, and they offer the additional advantage of showing facial expressions and body posture. In many ways, this makes them the next best thing to being there—though not everyone is comfortable with them or equipped to use them.

If you're physically distant from someone close to you and you want to offer condolences, you might try calling them by phone first then asking if you could do a video call with them soon.

IN A HANDWRITTEN NOTE

Personal letters and sympathy cards that include handwritten notes may be becoming rarer, but it seems this makes them even more treasured by those lucky enough to receive them.

I've included a section on sympathy card etiquette on the next page. But here I would just like to emphasize how meaningful it is for mourners to have the opportunity to savor your personal written thoughts. Face-to-face conversations and hugs are essential, but written words have the advantage of being keepsakes, available to be read and reread over and over again in the weeks, months, and even years to come.

Also, never underestimate the power of a long letter in which you share memories and personal anecdotes. As long as you keep in mind the guidance that follows about what to say and what not to say, an extended note of love and support is a generous, lasting gift of empathy and condolence.

SYMPATHY CARD ETIQUETTE

Sympathy cards are a more traditional and formal way to share your condolences than an informal text, email, or comment on social media. You might think of them as old-fashioned, but the truth is that they're a wonderful vehicle for giving condolences.

One of the best things about sympathy cards is that they're considered socially acceptable and nonintrusive no matter the type of (publicly known) loss or the sender. In other words, it's OK for anyone to send a sympathy card to virtually anyone else for virtually any reason. And those fortunate to receive them are almost always touched and grateful.

What's more, sympathy cards have a lasting impact. Understandably, most grieving people are shocked and numb during the early days after a significant loss. This time period is a blur, and it's often hard for grievers to remember what friends and family said when they visited or phoned. Sympathy cards, on the other hands, contain heartfelt messages that can be revisited whenever the mourner needs a dose of support. For many people they become cherished keepsakes.

Here at the Center for Loss, we believe that sympathy cards are so important that we even created our own line of "empathy cards." They're beautiful notecards that feature empathetic messages and avoid the "what not to say" phrases we'll review a bit later, including euphemisms and platitudes. If you're interested in learning more about our empathy cards, they're shown at the back of this book, and they're also available on our website, centerforloss.com.

So, yes—please do send or deliver a sympathy (or empathy!) card. Here's some etiquette to keep in mind:

- You don't need to buy a card designated as a sympathy card in the greeting-card section of a store for it to be considered a sympathy card. You can use any card you find appropriate. You can also use a blank notecard and write your own personal message.

- If you do purchase a designated sympathy card, the guidelines in this book will help you choose one that's most appropriate and empathetic. Always add a short, personal handwritten note of at least a sentence or two.

- If you don't know the person's mailing address, try looking it up on anywho.com or whitepages.com.

- Include your return mailing address on the card's envelope.

Mourners often want to keep in touch or send thank-you notes, especially to those who have also sent flowers, food, a donation, or another gift.

- If you're a reasonably close friend to the grieving person, or if you're a family member, it's best to think of a sympathy card as an additional way to let them know you're thinking about them. You should first visit them in person or call them. You can then follow up with a sympathy card.

- If you won't be visiting or calling immediately, it's most appropriate to send a sympathy card right away, when you first hear about the loss.

- If the loss has affected not just an individual but a family that lives in one household, address the card to the family. If you're closer to one family member, address the card this way: "John Smith and family." If you want to extend condolences to family members who live in different households, send each of them their own sympathy card.

- For a death, if you'll be attending a public visitation or funeral, there will usually be a basket placed near the entrance of the event location in which guests can deposit sympathy cards as they arrive. So if the visitation or funeral will take place soon after you receive news of the death, you can hang onto your sympathy card and bring it with you to this event. If the memorial service will be delayed for any reason, mail your card immediately instead.

IN AN EMAIL

Condolence emails can have much of the same impact as handwritten notes and sympathy cards—just without the look and feel of pen on paper. If you're more comfortable typing a longer email than writing a handwritten note—and you know that the recipient uses email regularly—this can be an effective option.

And keep in mind that you can mail a sympathy card with a brief note then follow it up with a longer email. Multiple contacts are a good way to be supportive, anyway.

IN A TEXT

Today, most people routinely send and receive texts as a form of daily communication with their closest friends and family members. Many are even comfortable using texting for the most personal, intimate conversations.

How you might use texting to extend condolences and ongoing empathy and support probably depends on your relationship with the person who is grieving. I would urge you to consider visiting in person and/or making phone calls first and using texting as a way of staying in touch in between more personal visits and phone calls. This applies, of course, only to grievers whom you know are comfortable with texting.

ON SOCIAL MEDIA

You might first learn about a friend or family member's loss on social media. Because they have the power to reach so many people in so many locations at the same time, platforms like Facebook have become common and socially acceptable places to share news of a death, divorce, job loss, miscarriage—any life transition that a person wants to let many others know about.

When this happens, don't hesitate to comment with your condolences. Be as supportive as you can in that forum, because the person who posted the news there is likely to be someone who will feel comforted by the immediate wave of support they receive. But if your relationship is close enough, it's also appropriate for you to follow up with a face-to-face visit or phone call. And remember that almost anyone can send a sympathy card—even if you don't know the recipient particularly well.

Also, be sure to follow the family's lead in using social media to share news of a death or give condolences. I've known families who first learned of a close loved one's death on social media, through a news story or an ill-timed post by a distant friend or family member. That's a terrible repercussion of the immediacy of social media. So please use caution, and ask the family before sharing any news or updates in this manner.

ON ONLINE MEMORIAL PAGES/GUEST BOOKS

After a death, you've probably visited online obituary and memorial pages on funeral-home and other tribute websites. These sites often allow you to write a brief comment to extend your condolences to the family of a person who has died.

When you are signing an online guest book, I encourage you to add at least a brief thought. I always think it's sad when I visit a page that contains almost no comments. Your thoughts are a way of chiming in as part of a chorus of concern. That's what we want mourners to feel—a community surrounding us with love and support. And as with the other first contact options we've reviewed, if you comment on an online memorial page, I encourage you to follow up with a sympathy card or email.

SHOULD YOU ALSO SEND FLOWERS, FOOD, OR A DONATION?

Especially in the immediate aftermath of a death, condolences and sympathy cards often go hand-in-hand with a gift of flowers, food, or a donation. Whether you choose to give such a gift will probably depend on your relationship with those who are grieving, how far away you live, and other factors.

But what I want you to keep in mind is that these gifts are also meaningful ways to express your empathy. They're really more symbols than tangible goods. They are physical representations of your care and concern.

Flowers (when culturally appropriate) are a good example. Today, more and more people misunderstand the role of flowers at a funeral. Again, think of them as representing you personally, especially if you can't be there yourself. When a casket or urn is flanked by numerous flower arrangements, this display represents an abundance of community support. What's more, flowers are beautiful and symbolize love and the fragility of human life. Consider contacting others whom you know would like to extend their condolences and sending a group floral arrangement from all of you.

Even if the family includes an "in lieu of flowers" message in the obituary, I hope you will still consider giving flowers (again, when culturally appropriate). Time and again I have seen these same families remark on how touched they are when they see the floral arrangements grouped together and bearing personal notes from supporters.

Of course, giving food to a grieving family is also a time-honored tradition. It can be hard to know if and when to provide food, however. Today, online tools like SignUpGenius allow friends and family members to coordinate edible gifts and meals so this support is spread out over time. You might also consider providing food a week or two after the loss instead of right away. In fact, families often appreciate receiving a gift of food months after a death. If you really want to show your support over the long-term, consider showing up with a homecooked meal several times in the coming months. If you prepare a food item that you know was special to the person who died or to this unique family, the griever will be especially touched by your efforts. And treats like homemade cookies are always welcome and can be dropped off or mailed anytime.

Donations in honor or memory of someone can also make heartfelt gifts, especially if you know of a cause or organization that was special to a person who died or is meaningful to the grieving person or family. You don't have to make a large donation for it to count. A modest gift, commensurate with your means, is more than enough. Remember, it's a symbol of your support more than it is a measure of your support.

Finally, it may be untraditional to give a gift of support after losses other than a death, but it can still be an appropriate, welcomed offering. When someone suffers a break-up, for instance, you could give them a blank journal or cleansing candle. A new empty nester might appreciate a spa gift card. A person who has had to move away from a beloved home might be comforted by a fun or silly care package.

Again, when it comes to gift-giving to grievers, it's more about the act of giving than the gift itself. The act conveys your care and concern, and the gift is a symbol. So give freely and often in small ways…and watch what happens.

WHAT TO SAY

"A letter of condolence may be abrupt, badly constructed, ungrammatical—never mind. Grace of expression counts for nothing; sincerity alone is of value."

— Emily Post

I hope I've convinced you already that saying or doing something—anything—is usually much, much better than avoidance. Reaching out with speed, compassion, and humility is all it takes to open the lines of connection.

As long as you are kind and withhold advice and judgment, you can say almost anything and the griever will interpret your condolences as well-intentioned. And remember—you don't always need words to acknowledge someone's grief. Sometimes a loving look, a gentle hug, or a touch of the arm is enough to let them know you are seeing them and present with them in their pain. So while I hope you will pick up a few "what to say" ideas from this section, please remember that it's OK to share what's in your heart in the moment.

WHEN YOU'RE SPEAKING WITH THE GRIEVER
When you're speaking with the griever in person or on the

phone, your goal in reaching out should be to express your condolences, yes, but more than that, to give the grieving person a safe moment in which to speak. Be brief, then let the other person talk. You can't go wrong to remember this mantra: mouth closed, ears open, and presence available. Or perhaps you'll resonate with this folk saying: God gave you two ears and one mouth. Use them proportionately.

Also, stay in the moment and honor the griever's current reality. Whatever they are expressing, you are there to bear witness to that expression. Allow them to steer the conversation. Use your active listening skills, and affirm back to them what you hear them saying. Help them feel heard and understood. You are there to receive, not so much to ask questions or express yourself.

If you are "feeling with" them, in empathy, it's OK for you to express emotion, too, or to offer to hold a hand or give a hug. When you are empathizing, your facial expression will likely mirror theirs. This is normal and natural.

What if you have questions or comments? If you've been letting them speak eighty percent of the time and the opportunity arises for you to ask an appropriate question or make an empathetic response, you can do so. But keep in mind that your own curiosity and need to understand may need to be reined in, especially in this initial conversation.

Finally, please remember to be sensitive. Even if you are well-intentioned, certain words and phrases can sometimes cut like a knife. Try to steer clear of the minefields listed starting on page 35.

WORDS TO OFFER

Human language is so inadequate in the face of great loss. That's why presence and empathy matter much, much more. But still, you have to say or write something! The following phrases and ideas are almost always well received by mourners.

For a written note or sympathy card, you will probably combine several phrases. If you're not sure how to get started, you might find this recipe helpful:

1. Say you're sorry about what happened:
   "I was so sorry to hear that…"

2. Then share a memory or say something about what was lost or about the griever:
   "David was such a loving person"
   or
   "I'll always remember the time…"
   or
   "I have always admired your…"

3. Close with an expression of comfort:
   "I'll be thinking of you"
   or
   "I'll call you next week."

- *I don't know what to say.*

  It's perfectly normal to be tongue-tied. It's OK to admit that out loud. Saying you're at a loss for words is sometimes the best way to convey your condolences. It gives the griever an opening to speak and for you to listen.

- *I just heard about _____, and I'm so sorry.*

  "I'm sorry" can seem trite and insufficient, but it does the job of conveying empathy. It lets the mourner know that you know that they are hurting. When expressed with genuineness, I believe it's a good, all-purpose condolence message.

- *I want to offer my condolences…*

  This is a more formal phrase than "I'm sorry," but it can be appropriate sometimes, especially if you're writing (versus speaking) a message and don't know the recipient well.

- *I'm thinking of you.*
  My thoughts are with you.
  You're in my prayers.

  You *are* thinking of them, so let them know that. When it comes to mentioning prayer, remember that this message is about the grieving person, not you. So use caution if you think they might be averse to religious comments.

- *My heart aches for you.*
  My heart goes out to you.
  My heart is heavy…
  This is another expression of empathy, and if it's true, it's a good one to use. You are letting them know that your heart hurts because it is empathizing with their heart, which is hurting.

- *When you're ready to talk, I'm ready to listen.*
  Letting the mourner know that you understand the importance of listening and are prepared to be an empathetic listener is a wonderful gift. But if you extend this condolence, don't sit around waiting for the mourner to contact you. Instead, reach out periodically and see if you can strike up a conversation. Then put on your listening ears.

- *You are so special to me.*
  (Name or relationship) was so special…
  Making a heartfelt compliment or observation about the grieving person can be an expression of empathy. This is a topic you can develop in a longer note. For example: "You have been such an important person in my life, and you've supported me in so many ways. (Give a notable example or two.) Now it's my turn to be there for you…"

You can also use this idea to talk about the special qualities you perceived in someone who has died, in the good days of the life of a person who is now ill or in a relationship that is ending, in memories of a relationship of place (a home, a neighborhood, a city) that is now changing, or in tribute to a beloved job or career that is now ending.

By letting the mourner know that you value them and/or that you see and appreciate the value of what they have lost, you are affirming their normal and necessary grief.

- *I'm here for you.*
  To be genuine and effective, this phrase should be considered a promise that must then be followed up by regular contact. Send the card, then a few days or a week or two later, reach out. The griever needs you to reach out to them, not the other way around. Avoid this phrase if you don't intend to actively reach out and stay in touch.

- *I want to help in any way I can.*
  Again, this phrase should only be used if you are committing to reaching out and offering specific help in the weeks and months to come. Grievers are often told, "Let me know if I can help in any way," but this is usually received as a hollow offer because grievers don't know how to act on it or feel it's too much of a burden to do so. Empty promises are worse than no promises at all. Nothing is worse than saying you will help or be in touch but then not following through.

- *(Share a memory.)*
  Mourners usually love hearing about special memories. For example: "I often think fondly of the weekend we spent…." Memories of the person who died or of past good times related to that which has been lost are also usually welcomed.

Finally, when you're thinking about what to say, remember that it's OK to be yourself, especially if you're speaking or writing to someone who knows you. You can be a little irreverent or humorous in certain circumstances, for example. It's better to sound genuine than to rely on clichés and platitudes.

HOW TO HANDLE CHALLENGING RESPONSES

Grieving people are deeply wounded, and occasionally some will respond to your well-intentioned overtures in unpredictable or aggressive ways. Please understand that these sideways or disproportionate reactions are usually not about you but instead about the profound pain they are suffering.

If a grieving person lashes out at you—even if you have said or done nothing to provoke it—try to have grace. Don't take it personally. Maintain empathy and seek to understand their experience from the inside out.

If, despite your best efforts, you end up saying something to a griever that upsets them, again—try to have grace. Apologize for not choosing the right words for them. Tell them that you feel for them and want to listen and help. Be humble, and let them talk. Let them rant and rave for a while if they need to (although if they're being abusive, it's absolutely appropriate for you to leave or discontinue the conversation).

If you can maintain your empathetic, calm presence during such an outburst, the griever will usually burn through their explosive emotions and begin to express the deeper, truer feelings underneath them—often sadness, hopelessness, regret, and despair. They will often apologize and, because you have remained steadfast during a stormy encounter, will begin to understand that you are someone on whom they can rely for support no matter what.

WHAT NOT TO SAY

"Speech has power. Words do not fade."
— Abraham Joshua Herschel

What not to say may be more important than what to say.
Try to avoid the following phrases. And if you find yourself
saying them anyway, or if you've used them in the past,
forgive yourself and try again. Our culture has taught you to
use them, and some are deeply ingrained. If you are earnest
and compassionate enough in your delivery, mourners
will often overlook phrases that they might otherwise
find wounding. And if you see that the mourner is upset,
apologize. Admit you've messed up and simply express your
desire to be of support to them.

- *I feel so angry/guilty/upset, etc.*
  Your condolence message should be focused on feeling
  with the grieving person—not your own particular grief
  over the loss. If you're someone who is mourning the same
  loss, it's perfectly normal to mention your own grief—just
  try not to make your outreach mostly about you. For
  example, if you know that both you and the mourner

share anger over a loss, it might be OK to mention this empathetic alignment, but in general, it's better to keep the focus on the mourner.

- *I know just how you feel.*
  Even if you've suffered a similar loss, you don't know. Not really. So take great caution in venturing into this territory, and be tentative, general, and brief if you do offer any such thoughts. For example, it might be OK to say, "Losing a parent is so hard. When my father died last year, I struggled for a long time." Later on, when you have the opportunity to have a longer conversation with the mourner, you will probably find it mutually beneficial to support each other over shared grief experiences. Still, keep in mind the rule of thumb to talk less and listen more.

- *I can't imagine what you're going through.*
  This is a common condolence phrase, but I find it disingenuous. With our innate human empathy, we automatically imagine what another person is experiencing. It's true that we can't truly crawl inside their consciousness to think and feel exactly what they're thinking and feeling, but we can and often do imagine what we might be experiencing if we suffered the same loss in our own lives. I recommend choosing a different message.

- *They're in a better place.*
  You must be relieved.
  It's for the best.

  It usually takes quite a while for mourners to reach this kind of conclusion for themselves (if they ever do). But shortly after a loss, in the here-and-now, they first need time to feel the void created by the loss and have others sit with them there.

  Sometimes mourners themselves will bring up this idea when they first communicate with you. It can be a way of minimizing their own grief, and our culture has taught them that they need to hurry up and "move on." So if you hear this from a mourner, try to be someone who doesn't encourage them to deny or bypass their own grief.

- *It was God's will.*
  Everything happens for a reason.

  These kinds of grand conclusions minimize mourners' own normal and necessary search for meaning. Mourners need time to discover what they think and feel about why things happen as they do. So over time, let them teach you about what they're realizing.

- *At least you…*

  At least you had ten good years of marriage. At least you have another child. At least you can try again. At least he's no longer suffering. These kinds of statements try to make the griever's loss seem smaller in the grand scheme of things. But it's up to the griever to decide and communicate to you how significant the loss feels to them. Don't minimize, rationalize, or compare. Don't start a sentence with "At least..."

- *Let me know how I can help.*
  It's good to offer your assistance—both practical and emotional—to people laid low by grief. They need your support. But this phrase is overused and typically under-committed to. People say it all the time but almost never follow through. Instead, be someone who follows up with the mourner regularly and suggests specific ideas to help. (See the section on what to do, page 41, as well as the suggested contact timeline, page 42.)

- *This too will pass.*
  Time heals all wounds.
  You'll be back to your old self in no time.

  Don't put a happy face on grief. Don't encourage mourners to skip over their pain. Don't promise rainbows and unicorns. Instead, be with the mourner and their authentic grief—whatever it is—in this moment.

AVOIDING PLATITUDES AND EUPHEMISMS

Many of the phrases in the "What not to say" section are harmful platitudes. A platitude is a statement about beliefs, morals, or values expressed in a clichéd way.

For example, the statement "It was God's will" conveys that God makes things happen and so we just have to accept them. The griever might believe neither of these things, and even if they do, it's not appropriate to encourage them to shortcut their grief.

Also try to avoid euphemisms. It's OK to be simple and straightforward. You can say "dead" and "died." Certain euphemisms, like "expired," "laid to rest," and "rest in peace," often feel jarring to grievers.

But there's also an important caveat when it comes to euphemisms. If the griever uses one, you can use it too. Matching their phrasing is a good way to convey that you're actively listening and empathizing. For example, if someone tells you that their grandpa "passed away," you'll know that you have permission to use the same term in talking or writing to them. Never correct their phrasing! There's nothing more obnoxious than a would-be supporter telling a griever what they should and should not say.

WHAT TO DO

"You can always give something, even if it is only kindness."
— Anne Frank

Here is what is really important to your helping efforts.

While it's absolutely essential to extend your genuine condolences shortly after a significant loss, it's also essential to follow up and to take ongoing action, especially if the grieving person is close to you and/or doesn't have an adequate circle of support.

I encourage you to continue to reach out and be a good listener. You really don't have to do anything more than that.

When you reach out, keep in mind the hierarchy of connection: Face-to-face is better than a phone call is better than an email is better than a text and so on. It's absolutely fine to use a combination of methods, but do try to make time for at least an occasional in-person visit or phone call. Invite the person out for coffee, a walk, or a sporting event. Stop by with flowers, if appropriate, or a pie.

When it comes to practical help, think about the little things that this unique griever may be struggling with since the loss. You might be able to babysit or help with pet care, for example. Or you can run errands or do yard work.

Don't be surprised if the griever lets you know that you're one of the few people staying in touch. Ongoing support in grief may be essential, but it's also rare.

A SUGGESTED CONTACT TIMELINE

You may feel unsure about when and how often to contact someone after a significant loss. The timeline that follows isn't at all firm but rather is intended to give you a general idea. Use your own common sense about frequency and methods of contact, but consider erring on the side of too frequent rather than too infrequent. Often, grievers are more or less abandoned by friends and family shortly after a loss.

If you're a busy person and you don't see the griever often, you might find it helpful to set reminders in your phone's calendar app. That way you can prevent too much time from accidentally slipping away in between contacts.

Within a day or two of the loss
Visit or call if you're close to the griever. Send a sympathy card or email if you're not.

Within a week of the loss
Send a sympathy card if you haven't already.

A few weeks after the loss
Call, email, or text to see how the griever is doing. Offer to meet up or help with practical matters if possible and appropriate.

A few months after the loss
Grief typically gets worse before it gets better. Be sure to reach out during this time period. Offer to meet up or help with practical matters if possible and appropriate.

On special occasions (such as birthdays and anniversaries) or during the holidays after the loss
Invite the griever to lunch or a gathering, call, or send a "thinking-of-you" card, email, or text.

On the one-year anniversary of the loss or another special day
Call, send another card or email, or text. Also consider sending flowers, if culturally appropriate.

On subsequent anniversaries of the loss or another special day
Call, send another card or email, or text.

A FINAL WORD

"Unless someone like you cares a whole awful lot,
nothing is going to get better. It's not."
— Dr. Seuss

Condolences are a gift of acknowledgment and compassion that you give to someone who is hurting. They are a way to tell those who have experienced a significant life loss or transition that you see them and you feel with them. You are not looking away from their pain. Instead, you are looking toward it—toward them—and you are bearing witness.

What's more, when we offer condolences, we're reminded of just how precious life is. We're invited to hold the mirror up to what gives our own life meaning and purpose. And that's a valuable opportunity, indeed.

There is nothing more important in life than making meaningful connections with others, and condolences are a crucial form of connection. They allow us to join hands and hearts when something comes to a close. As a culture, we are good at joining hands and hearts for beginnings. We are quick to extend congratulations for births, graduations, and weddings. But we're typically not so good at offering the same public affirmation and support at closing moments.

But you are helping rectify this. Thank you for being a condolence-giver and ongoing grief supporter. The world needs more of you.

TEN GUIDELINES FOR SHARING SYMPATHY AND CONDOLENCES

Please keep these in mind as you send your love and compassion out into the world.

1. *Think empathy.*
   Remember that empathy means joining with the feelings of the griever. You are trying to understand their experience from the inside out. It's about their unique feelings and experiences—not your feelings, assumptions, and experiences.

2. *Move toward the griever instead of away.*
   It's common for people to avoid grievers because loss situations often make us feel awkward and helpless. We don't know what to say or do. We think we can't say anything that will make it better. So we tend to say nothing. Yet grievers need their losses socially acknowledged and their grief supported. They need to feel seen and be heard.

3. *Be sincere—and yourself.*

   Let the griever know you genuinely care. As long as you convey authentic concern and compassion, it hardly matters which words you choose to say. And be yourself. Say things the way you would say them. Offer a touch or hug if that's part of how you show you care. Don't assume you have to be stiff and formal in giving condolences. Warm and real are much more effective.

4. *It's OK to be brief.*

   You don't have to say a lot. It's OK to be concise. But if you're sharing memories and compassionate, affirmative observations, a lengthy note or letter is a wonderful gift.

5. *Talk less, listen more.*

   If you're speaking to the griever, say a few words then be silent. Allow the griever to say whatever it is they want to say. You can be one of the few people who listen without judgment or the need to give advice. Gaps of silence are also OK.

6. *Steer clear of clichés and platitudes.*

   Grievers often feel dismissed by the clichés and platitudes they often receive. It's usually better to simply say "I'm so sorry…"

7. *Use caution with religious messages.*

   Condolences containing religious or spiritual beliefs or verses from the Bible or another sacred text may be

Sympathy and Condolences

comforting to some grievers but offensive to others. If you know the griever's beliefs, you can choose to align with them in your condolences. Otherwise, avoid religious sympathy cards and messages and instead stay here on earth with the griever.

8. *Be with the griever's pain.*
   It can be really hard to sit with someone who is feeling and expressing profound pain, but this is what grievers need most. They need your compassionate, nonjudgmental presence and active, empathetic listening skills.

9. *Follow up.*
   Grief is a long road, and it usually gets harder before it gets easier. It's important for supporters to follow up, when appropriate. The closer you are to the griever, the more often you should consider following up.

10. *Use what you're learning to accept condolences from others.*
    The better you become at expressing sincere condolences whenever the situation arises, and the more you learn to actively listen with compassion, the better prepared you will be to accept condolences with grace when the need arises in your own life. The more openly and honestly you will be able share your own feelings.
    By getting better at giving and receiving condolences, you will be helping create a more compassionate, kinder world.

Empathy Cards

Now instead of sending sympathy cards, you can offer your
empathy with these beautiful cards written by Dr. Wolfelt.
Where sympathy is passive pity, empathy strives to actively engage
and connect. Sympathy is "feeling for," while empathy is "feeling with."
Thank you for joining us in our mission to refashion our culture into
one of empathy rather than sympathy after a loss.

5-card set (5 different messages per set)
$10.00 • Includes white envelopes
Choose floral or canvas design • Notecards are 4.25" x 5.5"

Canvas Designs

Floral Designs

All Dr. Wolfelt's publications can be ordered by mail from:
Companion Press, 3735 Broken Bow Road, Fort Collins, CO 80526
(970) 226-6050 • www.centerforloss.com

Healing a Friend's Grieving Heart.

When a friend suffers the loss of someone loved, you may not always know what to say. But you can do many helpful, loving things.

This book provides the fundamental principles of being a true companion, from committing to contact the friend regularly to being mindful of the anniversary of the death.

ISBN: 978-1-879651-265 • 128 pages • softcover • $11.95

Finding the Words

It's hard to talk to children and teens about death and dying, particularly when someone they love has died or might die soon.

This practical and compassionate handbook includes dozens of suggested phrases to use with children of all ages as you explain death in general or the death of someone loved. Also included are ideas and words to draw on when discussing death by suicide, homicide, or terminal illness.

ISBN: 978-1-61722-189-7 • 144 pages • softcover • $14.95

Grief One Day at a Time

After someone we love dies, each day can be a struggle. But each day, if we work to embrace our normal and necessary grief and care for ourselves, we will also take one step toward healing. Those who grieve will find comfort and understanding in this daily companion.

ISBN: 978-1-61722-238-2 • softcover • 384 pages • $14.95

All Dr. Wolfelt's publications can be ordered by mail from:
Companion Press, 3735 Broken Bow Road, Fort Collins, CO 80526
(970) 226-6050 • www.centerforloss.com

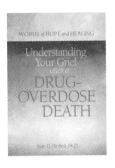

Understanding Your Grief After a Drug-Overdose Death

In this compassionate guide, Dr. Alan Wolfelt shares the most important lessons he has learned from loved ones who've picked up the pieces in the aftermath of a drug overdose. Readers will learn ideas for coping in the early days of their grief, as well as ways to transcend the stigma associated with overdose deaths. The book also explores common thoughts and feelings, the six needs of mourning, self-care essentials, finding hope, and more.

ISBN: 978-1-61722-285-6 • softcover • $9.95

Too Much Loss: Coping with Grief Overload

Grief overload is what you feel when you experience too many significant losses all at once, in a relatively short period of time, or cumulatively. Our minds and hearts have enough trouble coping with a single loss, so when the losses pile up, the grief often seems especially chaotic and defeating. The good news is that through intentional, active mourning, you can and will find your way back to hope and healing. This compassionate guide will show you how.

ISBN: 978-1-61722-287-0 • softcover • $9.95

All Dr. Wolfelt's publications can be ordered by mail from:
Companion Press, 3735 Broken Bow Road, Fort Collins, CO 80526
(970) 226-6050 • www.centerforloss.com

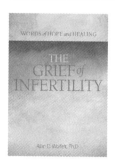

The Grief of Infertility

When you want to have a baby but are struggling with fertility challenges, it's normal to experience a range and mixture of ever-changing feelings. These feelings are a natural and necessary form of grief. Whether you continue to hope to give birth or you've stopped pursuing pregnancy, this compassionate guide will help you affirm and express your feelings about infertility.

By giving authentic attention to your grief, you will be helping yourself cope with your emotions as well as learn how to actively mourn and live fully and joyfully at the same time. This compassionate guide will show you how. Tips for both women and men are included.

ISBN: 978-1-61722-291-7 • softcover • $9.95

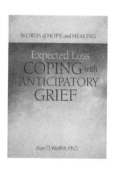

Expected Loss: Coping with Anticipatory Grief

We don't only experience grief after a loss—we often experience it before. If someone we love is seriously ill, or if we're concerned about upcoming hardships of any kind, we naturally begin to grieve right now. This process of anticipatory grief is normal, but it can also be confusing and painful. This compassionate guide will help you understand and befriend your grief as well as find effective ways to express it as you live your daily life.

ISBN: 978-1-61722-295-5 • softcover • $9.95

All Dr. Wolfelt's publications can be ordered by mail from:
Companion Press, 3735 Broken Bow Road, Fort Collins, CO 80526
(970) 226-6050 • www.centerforloss.com

Nature Heals: Reconciling Your Grief Through Engaging with the Natural World

When we're grieving, we need relief from our pain. Today we often turn to technology for distraction when what we really need is the opposite: generous doses of nature. Studies show that time spent outdoors lowers blood pressure, eases depression and anxiety, bolsters the immune system, lessens stress, and even makes us more compassionate. This guide to the tonic of nature explores why engaging with the natural world is so effective at helping reconcile grief. It also offers suggestions for bringing short bursts of nature time (indoors and outdoors) into your everyday life as well as tips for actively mourning in nature. This book is your shortcut to hope and healing…the natural way.

978-1-61722-301-3 • softcover • $9.95

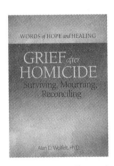

Grief After Homicide: Surviving, Mourning, Reconciling

Homicide creates a grief like no other. If someone you love died by homicide, your grief is naturally traumatic and complicated. Not only might your grief journey be intertwined with painful criminal justice proceedings, you may also struggle with understandably intense rage, regret, and despair. It's natural for homicide survivors to focus on the particular circumstances of the death as well. Whether your loved one's death was caused by murder or manslaughter, this compassionate guide will help you understand and cope with your difficult grief. It offers suggestions for reconciling yourself to the death on your own terms and finding healing ways for you and your family to mourn. After a homicide death, there is help for those left behind, and there is hope. This book will help see you through.

978-1-61722-303-7 • Softcover • $9.95

All Dr. Wolfelt's publications can be ordered by mail from:
Companion Press, 3735 Broken Bow Road, Fort Collins, CO 80526
(970) 226-6050 • www.centerforloss.com

NOTES:

NOTES:

NOTES:

NOTES:

ABOUT THE AUTHOR

Alan D. Wolfelt, Ph.D., is a respected author and educator on the topics of companioning others and healing in grief. He serves as Director of the Center for Loss and Life Transition and is on the faculty at the University of Colorado Medical

 School's Department of Family Medicine. Dr. Wolfelt has written many bestselling books on healing in grief, including *Understanding Your Grief, Healing Your Grieving Heart*, and *The Mourner's Book of Hope*. Visit www.centerforloss.com to learn more about grief and loss and to order Dr. Wolfelt's books.